SO-CON-709

# Bradford Washburn

## Jeri Cipriano

Boston, Massachusetts
Chandler, Arizona
Glenview, Illinois
Upper Saddle River, New Jersey

**Illustrations**
All illustrations: Timothy Jones

**Texts**
*The Last of His Kind: The Life and Adventures of Bradford Washburn, American's Boldest Mountaineer* by David Roberts. Copyright © 2009 David Roberts.

*Bradford Washburn: An Extraordinary Life: The Autobiography of a Mountaineering Icon* by Bradford Washburn and Lew Freeman. Copyright © 2005 Bradford Washburn and Lew Freeman.

**Copyright © 2013 by Pearson Education, Inc., or its affiliates.** All rights reserved. Printed in the United States of America. This publication is protected by copyright, and permission should be obtained from the publisher prior to any prohibited reproduction, storage in a retrieval system, or transmission in any form by any means, electronic, mechanical, photocopying, recording, or likewise. For information regarding permissions, write to Pearson Curriculum Rights & Permissions, One Lake Street, Upper Saddle River, New Jersey 07458.

**Pearson®** is a trademark, in the U.S. and/or in other countries, of Pearson Inc. or its affiliates.

ISBN-13: 978-0-328-67596-8
ISBN-10: 0-328-67596-2

3 4 5 6 7 V0FL 16 15 14 13 12

What do you love to do?

Bradford Washburn loved to climb.

When Washburn grew up, he went to Alaska to climb mountains.

He became famous among climbers.

Washburn was born in Massachusetts in 1910.

He had a younger brother named Sherry.

He and Sherry climbed snow hills together.

Washburn learned to fish in New York.

At the age of eight, he wrote an essay about it.

He liked to write about the outdoors.

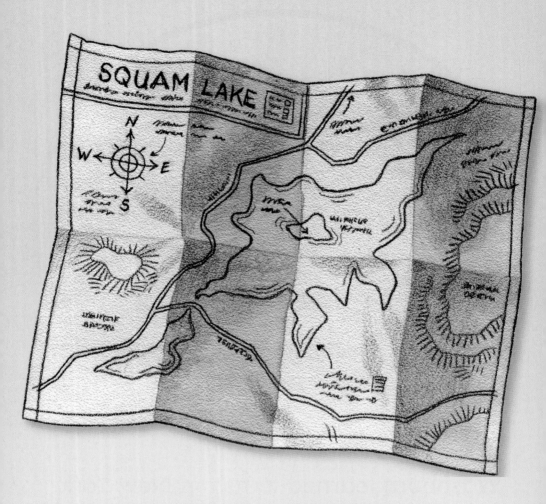

As a boy, Washburn liked maps.

He drew his first map at age 14.

It showed a lake in New Hampshire.

Washburn climbed his first mountain at age 11.

It was the highest mountain in the northeastern United States.

When Washburn was 16, his family went to Europe.

He climbed three huge mountains there.

Then he wrote a book about it!

At age 20, Washburn went to Alaska.

He tried to climb Mount Fairweather.

It is dangerous climbing mountains.

Climbers can die from the cold.

Mount Fairweather was difficult.

Washburn did not reach the **peak** that time.

In 1940, Washburn got married.

He and his wife went to Alaska.

They were the first people to climb Mount Bertha.

Washburn climbed many mountains.

He wrote books about his climbs.

"I was always a careful climber," he wrote.

Washburn also took **photographs** of mountains.

He did this from an airplane with one door removed!

Later in life, Washburn still worked in the outdoors.

He mapped the Grand Canyon.

He mapped Mount Everest in Asia.

Washburn was a hero to other climbers.

He taught people safer ways to **explore**.

He showed them the beauty of nature.

# Glossary

**explore** to go to places to learn more
about them

**peak** a mountain, or the very top
of a hill or mountain

**photographs** pictures taken by
a camera